NOT QUITE WITHOUT A MOON

IAN MCDONALD

NOT QUITE WITHOUT A MOON

NEW POEMS 2018-2021

PEEPAL TREE

First published in Great Britain in 2023
Peepal Tree Press Ltd
17 King's Avenue
Leeds LS6 1QS
UK

ISBN 13: 9781845235581

Printed in the United Kingdom
by Severn, Gloucester,
on responsibly sourced paper

CONTENTS

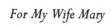
For My Wife Mary

ACKNOWLEDGEMENTS

My thanks to the following:

My grandchildren Jacob and Zoey whose joy in life continually delights me.

My sister Robin who never fails to help and encourage.

John Barnie whose letters on life and poetry matter greatly to me.

The memory of my parents whose loving presence has never faded.

I

MY MOTHER SINGS ME LULLABIES

Pain seized me; I cried out in horror.
Eighty years gone, his gold watch still swinging,
rotund Dr Littlepage still whispers I will die
unless I get to hospital. He will call the surgeon.
I woke from blackness after they had stifled me,
those white-coated torturers who tore me from my parents.

The cracked ice shone like diamond chips
in the silver spoon my mother placed against my lips,
tears glistening in her eyes like diamonds, too.
She brought mercy to my raging thirst.
I cried and cried for her, and she never left my side.
No visitors at night, they said, but her anger
struck them down. "You tie me up with ropes,
I will still come in." Beloved mother, such fierce beauty
I had never known. I knew then I would be safe forever.

THE SOUND OF MAKING BUTTER

Ram, the yardman, brought home
the frothing pails of milk
fresh as that morning's dew.
Soon I hear the soothing churn
of butter being made by hand,
sweetest I have ever known,
spread thick on homemade bread.

Antigua sea, on holiday,
the brave blue sound of waves,
the high wind in the cedar trees
on stormy nights of thunder,
my mother in the room next door
gently singing to herself
and I am inviolable for evermore.

RIPE MANGOES

A big night-wind shook the mangoes free
over the white sand beach below,
the red fruit fragrant harvest of the wind.
Sun hardly up, the old caretaker came
to fill a canvas bag with the produce of his realm.
Now and then he skinned a rich, ripe fruit,
juice dripping in his beard, a golden luxury.
I watched his enjoyment with my own delight.
Then, wonder of wonders, monkeys in the trees
began to make a racket against such thievery,
pelted the old man with branches broken off,
made an uproar and battled for their rights.
The bearded warrior must have been through this before;
strong arm aimed with accuracy, he pelted back,
chased a few who came down on the sand.
He won the battle, picked up the canvas bag
with a kind of flourish; they fled roaring in the trees.

THE LESSON

Sunday, the family picnicked at Macqueripe,
a small bay good for swimming and sandcastles.
I'd just learned to swim through my father's
thorough teaching. There was a place
where people went to dive; the sea deeper there,
dark green. "Let's see you jump in, son."
I didn't like it – too far out. I'd only swum in pools.
"You can do it, son. I'll keep my eye on you."
What could I do? I didn't like it, but he was my father.
I made up my mind, jumped in the deep green water.
I was all right. I surfaced, happy I had jumped,
surprised to find my father beside me, smiling.

VANISHED PALACES

When I was a seeking boy, I took my father's hand
in curious, quiet rooms in the museum;
images of tapestries, armour, goblets and old bibles
enthralled me in that marvellous world.
"Palaces have vanished into dust," my father said.
One thing I remember exactly – an ancient
Persian sword, scabbard scrolled in gold.
To this hour I recall the swirling red inscription:
"This sword killed a king and set a princess free."
Centuries of wonder blazed and never left me.

WALKING WITH MY FATHER

My father wakes me before the sun comes up;
we climb down to the little shell-strewn beach
below the cliff where sea-scented winds blessed
us all day long when we stayed for our holidays.
We walked along the coast, waves around our feet.
Sometimes we saw the sun rise marvellously blood-red
amid black horizon clouds, glowing veins of gold.
Sometimes fishermen passed with lobster pots
and my father bargained with them if the catch was fresh.
He talked with me so much, whatever caught his fancy,
things puzzling and strange – I never found it boring.
Eleven years of age, my mind easily caught fire –
war and peace, life and death, invading Nazis in Europe.
Excitement in his voice, history's sweep he spent
some time explaining. He was a quiet man,
but he could tell a story. Years have lengthened
into lives since we walked together but I remember how
he thrilled to tell the storming of the beaches,
of cricket heroes, books to read, of the sugar factory
where he worked, years alone in England
and the cocoa-plant research he'd done
at Imperial College; doctor Grandpa's surgery,
the poems Grandma wrote. In later years I had
much more to say. He listened well, so I
found our walks an adventure among the splendours
of the morning sky, the changing colours
of the sea, moments of nature's thousand gifts.
How could I forget the albatross soaring along the heights
of heaven, exulting? From him I came to sense
the wonders of creation on those walks along Antigua's coast
so long ago. And then the joy of coming back
to find my mother's breakfast feast waiting on the table:
fried chub cutlets, fungi cakes, scrambled eggs, just so.

MANGO PICKING AT ONE CARMODY ROAD

The winds of life have blown the years away;
our lovely St Augustine home vanished long ago.
Happiest of families, we lived the happiest of times.
Who can deny what none of us will doubt?
Tears fall to think that not a trace remains,
but now and then moments come in dreams:
my father and my mother in the upper garden.
He climbs a laden mango tree, looks out,
throws down ripe fruit my mother does not catch.
He laughs and she complains with such a lovely look
her beauty catches at my heart. The love
between them gave certainty to all our lives.
"You need to practise catching, love," he says.
"Oh you don't throw them properly," she replies.
He drops down from the tree. They hug and laugh.
The dream dissolves but when I wake they live.

GROWING UP

Eighty years have passed and still
I remember the sweet wind in my face
racing down the hill in St Augustine
lined with red-fruited pomerack trees.
Daring and dangerous, faster than I could run,
I, jubilant and free on my heroic bike,
flew past strangers turned to look.
It was such a good feeling, my father's hand
no longer on the saddle – loving teacher, cautious
and controlling – going faster than he would ever
allow. Now only I could know,
just before the intersection at the bottom,
how many times I braked just in time.

BEHEADING A CHICKEN

He beheaded the chicken,
the village boy I knew so well.
Shocked, I did not close my eyes.
Blood gushed on the tree stump,
black eyes would not close.
I knew there was suffering.
Casual, he didn't think about it.
Images jostle in my mind,
of a life I consider good.
I want to get rid of that one.
Write it; perhaps it will go away.
Spit out a gulp of mind-shit —
what else, now I've started, what else?

WILD FLOWERS

Everywhere that day there were wild flowers.
Racing before the rain-storm, laughing,
we came to this old disused barn,
pushed the door off its hinges, crowded in.
It smelled of cocoa and rat-droppings —
eighty-years smell-memory never fails.
We arm-wrestled, played pocket-chess,
talked of cricket, girls and art.
The wind grew tremendous,
great cracking sounds silenced us completely.
We rushed to get out, desperate, shouting.
In minutes, we watched the barn blown down,
laughing, drenched in the shelter of the sky.

PRAYER

Once when I was a young boy
with my friends hunting butterflies –
so many in those days, tint-bright and lively –
we went to the abbey on Mount St Benedict.
Refreshed ourselves with water as we always did –
so good its cold after the noonday sun.
I wandered in the silent abbey for a moment:
a single monk on his knees in prayer,
head bowed, hands grasped together tight,
now and then looked up, so grave a look –
Christ dying on the cross in shining wood.
I saw the monk was near as young as me,
saw teardrops of blood carved red on Christ's figure.
All that time ago; the image is steadfast.

THE FROG

I am telling this exactly as it happened:
a young boy of sixteen, sheltering in a small shop
by Tunapuna, rain pouring out of evil-looking clouds,
a big grey frog on the dirt road outside flopped
slowly across, taking its time – slow big hops.
A few cars went by just missing it.
I watched a while – miss, miss – then ran out,
nudged the frog, kicked it gently to safety
in my khaki shorts, t-shirt ringed like a tiger,
soaked to the skin. Nobody sheltering
with me said anything except a young man
who looked at me smiling. "Man," he said, "man."

GREAT-AUNT ANNA

My great-aunt Anna never married;
they said she loved me like an only son.
Every night she said her jewelled rosary
to protect me so I never need to worry.
I would be safe, pass exams, win the tennis.
I went away, didn't see her for years —
the ceremony of blessing when I left was sad.
She wrote me once to say she said her rosary
every night and day. I was not to worry —
all written in her curving hand.
When at last I saw her, she was far gone.
They said, "Her mind has wandered from its moorings."
I don't know if she knew I'd visited.
Her eyes blind in the quiet, her old
veined hand held mine tighter, tried to tell me
something about when she was young.
How when she was just a little girl
she'd climbed a tree, deep into its green branches,
and it was beautiful there in the green tree.

TEA WITH UNCLE ARTHUR

So like my beloved father, his young brother –
short-clipped, grey abundant hair,
how he leant slightly against the wind,
crinkling lines about eyes that had seen Antiguan sun –
their brothers' look: steady, clear and kindly.
We went for tea and talk at the Copper Kettle.
My first term at Cambridge – I was very young.
He'd been asked, I'm sure, to check my settling in,
for true, I was not only young but a little lost.
I liked him very much at once, and always afterwards;
not for one moment stiff with fame at all,
though he had made his mark upon the world,
had helped beat Hitler in the great Battle of the Air;
history will know him, but he would never tell.
In the Copper Kettle we talked and laughed.
He mentioned Hazlitt and found I knew him well,
quoted him – perhaps he had it planned and ready –
"Much thought on hard subjects after time
stems and dulls the dancing of the spirits,
the gaiety of mind and weighs upon the heart,
so making us disremember what we are about
enjoying every day's common sweet pursuits."
He told me I must relish life without the lecture.
"If you have any trouble, come to me,
and even more if you have none at all."
With a sudden pang, I recognise the familiar smile.

FOREST AT NIGHT

Once the forest caught me in the night
looking for orchids. The sun was going
down fast, green, cool sunlight slanting in.
Tangled vines underfoot, with flowers
in between, like jewels; branches
marvellously interlaced like ceilings.
Panic. I could no longer see the trail ahead,
feared black jaguars waiting in the black night,
the slippery noise of snakes in the black leaves,
great boles of trees a blacker shade of black.
Suddenly, against the half-moon,
a golden hawk burst flying in the sky,
shone through the fretwork of the forest canopy.
All was well. I knew my way ahead,
black knives of imagination quickly put away.

AMEN

Hard rain overnight. Clouds scudded
at dawn across a mottled sky. Fierce wind –
a knife between its teeth – stormed in the trees.
I decided, contrariwise, to take a long swim
out to the sandbank, the tide tugging me.
I was a strong swimmer – got there safe.
Stayed awhile, colour of blood in the sky.
Saw how some birds struggled against the wind,
how others used it, soaring gracefully.
I'd wanted to do that for a long time.
If I'd had a good voice, I would have sung;
I spoke 'The Windhover' – what I could recall –
then shouted loud as I could, Amen.

PLACE OF WORSHIP

Across the golden wheatfields I see again
Chartres' unusual spires soar gloriously to heaven.
Within, I worshipped not so much God, as beauty
bathed in radiant colours as I knelt below.
Now, a different place, a chapel near the sea,
comes to mind: rough wooden walls
built on green Antiguan stone,
big enough for a village's Sunday needs.
Path of shells and coral took you up to it.
In the lively wind you could hear the waves.
I went in to pay respects, my first time passing by.
A simple wooden altar, bare of all adornment,
Jesus roughly carved, thorns thick upon His head.
Three nuns in black habits knelt at the altar rail,
no cushioning upon the hard, plain wooden floor.
No one else was in the place. I also knelt in prayer.
Three frail old women in silent adoration:
I felt the goodness of the world surprise me.

CONCERNING MY FATHER AND MOTHER

I never made a point of telling them
how much as parents they meant to me,
always treated me with love,
praised me, never put me down,
discussed with me the doubts I had,
backed me up when I'd decided.
Once, I'd lost the first set in the finals
of the junior championship I'd set my heart on.
From the stands my father signalled
and from then I knew I'd win.
His and my mother's love –
no conditions were attached.

In Antigua, when they were very old,
at Cliff House, home of such great beauty,
they talked with me of a thousand memories
until a gold sky turned to night,
then they walked hand-in-hand towards the house.
I followed up the shell-strewn path,
thinking how much I'd always loved them.
Just then they turned as one and smiled,
as if my voice had spoken to them.
Perhaps it did. I write it now.

BLACK FLAMINGOS

"You're right to wake me, my son,"
my father said, "from an old man's endless doze."
"Come see the clouds at sunset," I invited,
"a blaze of red, shot through with silver-black
flamingo-shapes whirling in the wind.
This is unusual, you must see it."
I told him the story of Giotto di Bondone,
great artist, who once saw spittle stains
on walls blue and white that
"conjured up fantastic births and adorations",
who made outrageous beauty from a beggar's spit.
"When I was young, I watched the clouds," he said.
My beloved father, you are never old,
I can take you to see the clouds of heaven.

II

EYES THE COLOUR OF ICE

Unforgettable omens that day
I had asked to meet him –
such was his fame and mystery –
swarms of blue-winged moths,
sun molten-gold in a pitch-black sky,
birds shrieking from a far wilderness,
campfire crackling near the river's edge.
Gold gleaming on his bunched fist,
he smiled and shook my offered hand,
spoke in a cultured voice. Everyone was quiet
to hear this black man with those blue, fair eyes.
A wounded jaguar tracked, he said,
led him to the gold rocks of his fame.
They came to rob him soon enough,
the big men of the river claims.
He lifted up the golden knuckle-dusters:
"I battered out their brains."

THE GREEN-EYED OWL

Being told of him and having seen his wondrous jaguar head,
I made a pilgrimage to meet the supreme carver,
far up Santa Rosa Creek off the Demerara river,
where spring water bubbles cold and clear.
From a ramshackle house midst bamboos creaking in the wind
he greets me, as if I was an old and treasured friend,
a gaunt man with toothless gums, one eye clouded blue,
lean, young-looking fingers stained with berry juice.
He showed me his gleaming knives, also a jewelled gouger
an Englishman gifted him when he was very young.
"I work with the heart of trees." He looked beyond me;
his unseeing eye saw into the unity of things:
the fruit, foliage, flowers, shells and flying birds he fashioned.
On that day, when I looked up, the blue went on forever.
In that time of magic, I bought a masterpiece
my descendants will treasure for a thousand years:
small as my hand and wrist, a green-eyed owl
emerging from shone purpleheart, eye-socketed in jade.
Look, every feather's ruffling in an eternal wind.

THIS MAY MATTER

Give attention to these lines.
It's important that you see
what I never have forgotten.
One evening, on the Parika road,
I stopped at a shop for cold cane juice,
spicy potato balls to take away.
A tower of a man seated on a stool,
sweaty after toil, sipped an ice-cold beer,
in his other hand, twiddling, twiddling,
bright sky-blue macaw feathers.
Quiet, gazing into the distance of his life.

THE TEXAS MULE STAMPEDE

Texas mules for transport in the sun-burned fields –
the last consignment in the history of sugar –
arrived at Thom and Cameron, centre of the city.
Sweating stevedores somehow got them on the wharf –
the long sea voyage made them good and testy –
in storage pens for the estates to collect them.
Mid-morning, no way these pens could hold
mad-vex Texas mules. One big commotion,
the irate mules burst out, smashing pens to smithereens,
gloriously stampeding through crowded shopping streets
in the city's centre. At first it was sensation, then pure fun,
people pointing, laughing, young ones giving chase.
Soon a bounty was offered for every mule recovered.
Sharp haggling – of course, every captured mule was Texan!
Records show they scattered far and wide:
Liliendaal, Sophia, Ogle, Industry, Mahaicony.
All caught, except three. Great events have taken place
in our nation's history – visits by royalty, parades
of winning teams, revered presidents laid to rest
in funeral processions – momentous and memorable
in their time and place, but none lives as long in song and story
as when Texas mules went rampaging through our city.

END OF CROP BONUS

On the way down from the Berbice estates,
in a rum shop, drinking cold beer, after a long hard day,
four sugar workers sat at a table nearby,
ash-dirty from the fields with their bags and cutlasses,
a big bottle of D'Aguiar's rum in their midst.
My mind flashed: What truths do these men consider?
They talked (not loud, I heard the seriousness) of the crop bonus
decided at the Board earlier that week,
discussing how to spend it. I was surprised.
Childrens' schoolbooks, clothes, shoes, a new bicycle.
One said he would get his wife glasses.
I was ashamed to be taught such a simple lesson.

BLUE PLUMBAGO HEDGE

One day the manager at Albion estate
replaced the blue plumbago hedge
all around the factory compound
with flaming red bougainvillea.
Asked why, "Boredom," he said.

RESETTLEMENT: A BETTER LIFE FOR SUGAR WORKERS

We were inspecting run-down logies at Industry,
deciding the fate of sugar workers.
A better future we planned – decent housing.
Getting information about numbers in the families,
out of the corner of my eye I saw her,
a little girl about three, lustrous-eyed and shy,
long dark plaits dancing down her back,
red ribbons tied so carefully, so lovingly.
She peeped-out curiously. I could not help but note
a large belly on her, strange and ugly.
Hardly believing it could be hunger, I asked.
No, she sick, big tumour growing, growing bigger.
What could I do? No, this has no happy ending.
Nothing could be done, nothing tried.
A year or two later they got the new housing,
roads, running water. I suppose better lives.

ii

We visit this older lady – pillow breasts, thick hair
mostly grey in black – in her little shack –
yes, shack – though she keeps it well and neat:
small room and a smaller kitchen space.
Calm-eyed, unagitated, she smiled a lot.
She's sorry she has only one sweet drink to offer two of us.
She's widowed, her husband had been very good.
She has a small allotment for her use elsewhere –
mostly herbs she used and sold and gave away –
a few chickens in a pen next door.
People were kind; they helped. She could manage life,
she minded little children for people doing work –
she hugged a few who scampered around us.
People said she intervened in quarrels when asked;
she had a hundred remedies, good reasoning as well.

Auntie Deygoo distress nobody.
She always find a way.
She makes provision for herself.
She is happy with her lot in life.
She binds wounds and has solutions.
Neighbours respect her far and wide.
She gathers little children kindly round her.
Put this case aside – how does one resettle love?

THE EXAMPLE WE MUST SET

Once I chaired a tribunal of three,
to decide a man's employment future.
Simple case: he was a good worker,
years of devoted service, always on time,
not a high-flyer, without fail reliable,
but he had taken money from the till.
No doubting facts; he simply asked forgiveness.
No, my colleagues said, we can't set a precedent.
Everyone knows it'll happen all the time.
For that alone we must set an example.
He came before us, sad and old and wordless.
I had this feeling about him – recommended mercy.
My colleagues didn't like it, though they liked me,
knowing I'd never be chief executive. Never was.

WILLY KONG TING

Thursday mornings, my mother ordered groceries,
made her list sitting by the telephone.
I gave her my own list sometimes, mostly sweets,
Jacobs ginger biscuits – dates I also loved.
Willy Kong Ting owned a little shop,
he came backdoor once, begging for our custom.
Thursday morning, religiously, he got our mother's order.
Early afternoon he returned, his cycle fully laden,
big front basket piled high with all our groceries.
Two trips or more he made – whatever the order needed –
rain or shine all the same, never knew him sick.
My mother never questioned him, always paid the bill,
got to know his big smile and the extra sweets.
She liked Kong Ting's Grocery Express very much.
After years of loyalty and toil, he got a small new van,
proudly drove me in it before I went abroad.
Decades later, Kong Ting's Super Market
challenged the best there was in central Trinidad.
A grand opening and I was visiting at the time,
so we all went, and seeing us, Willy abruptly left
the mayor and all the dignitaries, greeted us,
bowed low to our shy and flustered mother
and brought her, not us, with ceremony to a place
of high honour. We knew she was beloved.

THE BLUE DRESS

At the Cathedral of the Sacred Heart,
before it burnt on that sad Christmas Day –
crib straw catch fire from a holy candle –
there was this old lady, always at the door
for Sunday evening mass; she was allowed to beg.
She'd say, "Please for a dollar, a penny will do."
I remember that, even after the big devaluation,
nothing else: "Please for a dollar, a penny will do."
Except that one-time shock when she looked me straight:
"Mister, you give a nice blue dress, mine old?"
I bought a nice one for her with lace cuffs.
She shrugged, put it in a paper bag.

SIXTY YEARS AT BOURDA

Match time at Bourda pavilion, I was always there
to sit next to old man Spencer, veteran of memories.
Sixty years – by now he had a special chair,
knew all the greats, unfolded all the dramas.
He had no equal for stories and statistics.
I loved to listen, a soft lilt in his voice,
as he remembered every century, all 10-wicket hauls.
Lance, that fierce off-spinner, he most of all revered.
"I never see him less than fight tooth and nail."
The time came when he befriended me, talked about himself –
retired after fifty years managing in shipping.
His whole life was cricket though, never missed a day.
"I had a strict routine, you know, always brought my tea."
Strange, I recall, with so much else worth the telling,
that brown bread soaked in honey he shared with me.

THE THROW

(For Joe Solomon on his 90ᵗʰ birthday)

"Tension in the gut like knife, skipper say stay calm.
Wes bowl, Kline play, my fellow fielder dash –
young Peter in a rush to run Ian Meckiff out.
All to play for – good Test becoming great.
I know it is historic; they have one run to win
and we Windies could still save the day.
I know I is a quiet man, but I was born for this.
Was in me the desire, the glory or the loss.
Body, mind and soul took aim. 'Leave it to me,' I say."

Well past ninety when she first wrote to me
on yellow foolscap, spiky, but well spelt,
plain clear what she had to say.
"Every Sunday, you write beautifully."
Warm praise with shrewd and decided views.
She wrote regularly. I have a sheaf of notes,
poems she sent – including Frost's apple-picking verse.
It astonished me to see Walcott's 'Egrets' quoted;
I could not think how she could come across the lines.
I replied to all her notes with abundant thanks,
wrote with care how valuable I found her views,
how interesting I found the story of the life
that she unfolded: English school-girl to colonial wife –
her husband ran the Mazaruni Prisons.
What tales she told of life up Essequibo,
the window where she watched the mighty river
"in all its moods of beauty". I imagined all night
star-bursts in the heavens. A pity she was old
and could not tell me more. Her spinster daughter,
who now lived with her in town, told me
she still mourned the son whom the Great War killed –
they never found him. She did not amplify.
Forty years a widow, his smile she still remembered,
serious in the uniform she laid out for him each day,
gave detailed descriptions of the Mazaruni gardens
where old prisoners helped her with devoted hearts.
Her last letter said she had a thousand memories,
but they were fading fast and she was weary.

. . .

"No use visiting, sir. She's completely deaf,
deaf as greenheart," her daughter said.
But still I visited. Who would not go
at least this once to mark the hundred years?
She smiled; her eyes were ageless, so bright

they shone an inner light. On a black rocker,
bright cushions around her, fragrant white dress,
blue-laced at cuffs and neck, black boots,
she touched the rocker up and down,
greeted me with thanks for my trouble coming.
"Your writing gave my soul relief."
She took my hand; bone-sharp fingers tightened.
I smiled and took the offered seat,
conveyed in notes what I wished to ask –
easier than you think to make such conversation –
slow's not awkward when "Patience is a virtue".
The daughter served Earl Grey and dainty sugar cakes
on bone china, a wedding gift "a thousand years ago."
When I saw she was tired, I took my leave with thanks,
rose with smiling courtesies, waved farewell at the window,
a moment in my life I'll not easily forget.
Not long afterwards she died. She had sent a last letter,
scribbles to me that were not readable,
but she had tried, and I tried hard to read them.

· · ·

Black-suited at the funeral, I murmured praise;
hesitant, I found it hard to find good words.
A few people in the dusty parlour whispered
near the plain-wood coffin – which was shining.
Who sent the one red rose? Not me.
I spoke about the letters, how much they meant to me,
quoted Walcott's "Season...", wished her eternal peace.
The burly pastor proclaimed her beloved of the Lord
and a dark wagon came to get the nothing she now was.
In the bright sun I stumbled out, not seeing very well.

FISHING FOR PATWA

Coming home from an early morning walk,
I came across a little boy, seven or eight,
fishing in the trench that runs near our home,
lilies on the surface out in all their glory,
his rod a crooked tree limb, I don't know about the hook.
He'd caught a few patwa, put them in a pail.
He wore a cap. Somehow I remember it had a jaunty angle.
I asked, "How you doing?" pleasantly I hope.
He didn't look at me, perhaps he thought I was
accusing him of trespass. "I'm not stopping you," I said.
Then he looked at me; his brown, frightened eyes
made me very sad. He was there to get him
and his mother breakfast. "Don't bother. Here is
nough-nough money. Take it easy; this is for
your mother's food." I gave him a lot of money,
not feeling very good, put it near the pail, then went away.
A little later, from the window I saw he was fishing still.
He'd picked a few white lilies and put them by the pail.

ANGELS WILL LOOK AFTER HIM

Walking with nine-year Jacob, evening sun aflame,
along the seawall where it first was built,
it was good talking about why the wall was there:
"Look how the land is far beneath our feet."
The vastness of the sea was another subject:
"What we know is just a thimble of the ocean."
Then afar, an old man I could see was crazy
strode towards us, blood-glaze in his staring eyes;
gesturing to the sun, his lips opened in a roar:
"Oh sun blaze fury-red before the day is done."
Exactly that he uttered – how could I forget?
I put Jacob the safe side of me as the old man passed.
Close up, he seemed to have devoured stones;
his mouth agape, you saw the bloodied gums.
Quietly he passed us, not a sign of rage,
My grandson silent. Then he said to me,
"I am sad for that old man, he looks so bad.
He has no teeth, Granddad, what will happen now?
Will angels look after him?" I held him to my heart.

III

MY BELLY GROWS ON ME

Getting fat with age – a lack of moving well –
having to alter the girth of my blue trousers,
favourite work pants for walking in the garden,
I sent them to an old tailor in Forshaw Street
to try him out. Days later, passing his cramped shop,
I went in the shuttered room. He sat above
a cut-scarred bench, old-man hunched,
bent as a hammered nail. I noticed his long, tough fingers,
silver-threaded small goatee, brown and brilliant eyes.
Turning to me, he gave a gold-toothed grin,
"Sit here, just now I finishing your piece."
I watched him in his deft and daily work,
take up my trousers, cut the waist to lengthen it
with quick-silver scissors, then peddled the Singer
black and gold, did the job so quick.
"I never did something so well in all my life," I said.
This pleased him. "This should suit your belly, boss-man,"
he smiled, "until this time meet next year at least."
We punched fists, laughed. Some men you love at once.

JOINT PAINS

Memory fresh as marigolds by moonlight:
I am a boy wielding a toy sword,
jousting with an ox-strong kid next door,
his hair a flame of orange, I recall.
He cracked me on the knuckles hard,
laughed and cracked me hard again.
Blood-bruised, it hurt but I was too old to cry.
Woke this morning a lifetime later,
my right-hand knuckles stiff with pain.
Joints crack and hurt, but I remember
at least he did not thrust me to the heart.

NOTHINGNESS

I attended a big funeral –
duty really, not someone I knew.
A trade unionist, man of the people.
Many dignitaries were there;
the bishop delivered a moving eulogy;
there was a woman in a black veil
who wept for him. I felt real sadness.
But what I remember best by far:
a little girl in pigtails saying quite loud,
"Has he just gone into nothing?"

THE GRANDCHILDREN ENQUIRE ABOUT MY DEATH

Of course, I will still be around.
I love you very much – always will.
Those who love you always stay around
somewhere, you can be sure of that.
Happy or sad or good or bad or medium,
I'm going to be taking a big interest in you.
Remember I'll still be in the universe,
and you know that no part of the universe ever dies.
All the time you are growing up, getting old even,
I'll be around keeping an eye on both of you.
The important thing is I love you very much,
so I'll be around, you can be very sure.
Things like hugging me around my neck,
or running away faster than I can catch you?
You may not be doing these things, that's true,
but you know that what you think and feel
inside you means as much as what you do outside of you,
and inside you is where you will always find me.
Everything will be well, don't worry yourselves.
Now come and hug me tight around my neck.

THE LAST DANCE

It is long, long ago,
forty-one years to be precise.
I am now very old;
she seems young to me
but she isn't, I suppose.
I remember the first time
I realised something.
Said to her at the party:
I want the last dance.
She said yes you can.
I will always want the last dance,
I said, and she smiled.

"I WILL NOT LET YOU DIE, MY LOVE"

For long the days darkened in my life;
breath was hard to get, weakness stilled the limbs,
effort made no sense, world a-tilt, wild colours in my head.
She never failed, my Northern Star, my love.
I grasped her shoulder getting to the garden;
one hundred songbirds in their beauty greet me,
alighting in the tree's green and golden branches,
their gleaming wings glimmering in the wind.
Their throats of silver poured forth such music
I was moved to wonder and to tears of love.
So good again to breathe sweet air and live.

THE SILENCE OF GOD

Storm of rain and wind scoured the earth
all yesterday and through the night, the morning
crystal bright, the new day quiet, breathless waiting.
Night comes again and I see there is no moon.
Suddenly, it seems to me, now's a good time.
I know the presence of God this still, black night –
kept the thought to myself, not for sharing.
I go out in the garden near midnight hour,
walk slow in complete quiet, then decide
to lie full length on the soft grass on my back,
under the great breathless trees as old as me,
an endless heaven strewn with pearls;
I have never seen such a river of stars.
I do not remember how long I stayed there,
thought about what might be created or discovered.
A trillion years will pass, it came to me.
I rose at last and sank upon my knees.

MOTHER AND SON

From dusty storage in Antigua
I hold a portrait just as old as me,
now closing in on eighty-six.
I can hardly believe how beautiful and young
she looks, cradling her first-born in her arms,
smile of love and triumph in her eyes,
head tilted as I at once recalled,
my ancient heart hurting to remember
the confidence and love she made a part of me.
Tears sting though I resist them.
Young mothers never think
of sons grown old and dying.

THE GREY MOUNTAIN

Old friend, the grey mountain looms.
You will climb it first, it seems,
its cliff steep and hard as iron.
Ascent will be a desperate thing;
it would be good if I could help,
between us deal with this fierce thing,
talk this through as we have done
so many times. "What else?" we said.
I'll get you past the Larkinian fear
there's nothing more to hope for.
Time in the end alone we know;
soon enough that fades to nothing.
We have spoken of this too.
Let me believe for both of us
that the darkest of all summits can be won.
What is immortal brightness like?
What strange tales, what wondrous things?
Wait there awhile for me, old friend.
Soon come. I'll want to talk.

THE LEMON TREE

Here it is again, the marvellous morning light,
rain-washed air freshened by the breeze.
I remember gold-eyed egrets standing in green fields,
grass green and soft as gleaming river moss,
and here they are again after all these years.
They have not stirred, they share eternity with me.
I was not well at all, I was near death;
my love had brought me home again,
one last time perhaps. I had come out in the morning
and there the old beauty is. Thirty years have gone,
the wind rises and I smell the jasmine flower,
and I hear her say, "Long long ago for you, my love,
I planted a lemon tree; there it is for you,
thick-leaved now, heavy-fruited, sweet-blossomed."
In our heaven it has grown. Time passes,
but beauty does not pass, and love does not.

I KNOW WHEN I AM DYING

I know when I am dying
I will praise the beauty I have known,
the blessings of the passing days
the wonder, the heaven-spray of stars.
I know when I am dying
I will praise the travelled world,
the sun dawning on strange mountains,
the moon racing in wild storms,
the surging stallions of the sea.
I will praise the glorious cities
where I found so many friends.
I will praise the infinite store
of all the wisdom I have touched,
the truths I tried so hard to learn.
I will praise the kindness shown me,
bravery against power that is hard.
I will praise those who helped the poor.
I will praise the children;
their joy in life has fulfilled me;
may their days shine forever
as my days have shone for me.
I will praise the great river –
we swam there that first morning,
you sleek as a seal, eyes shining,
welcoming me into your arms.
Above all, I know my heart.
I know when I am dying
I will praise you, my dearest,
I will praise your love.

IV

HER TASKS DONE WELL

She goes downstairs to gather flowers in the sun;
she does not see that I am watching her;
such a lovely thing – my world is calmed.
Slowly she goes from bed to bed choosing flowers
carefully for colour and for beauty,
humming to herself, brushing back her hair.
Now she bends and digs out tough weeds,
puts them in a special bag for garden rubbish.
Ah look, she screens her eyes to watch the parrots fly.
She goes over to the herb beds, has the scent of them.
I can almost smell them, too, breathing deeply.
How good this is watching her in the flowers,
digging out the tough weeds, smelling the herbs,
with separate baskets for flowers and herbs.
Then she sits in the shade of the orchid house,
rests awhile, wind in the trees above her.
She doesn't stay long, she is always hard-working.
Her mother told her, day after day, never waste time.
I can see she is happy with what she has done,
wanting to come up to fix the flowers, pack the herbs.
I'll greet her with golden apple juice, well chilled,
share some time to look at the beauty of the flowers.
She will not know how completely content I am
to have seen her pick the flowers, gather the herbs,
sit by herself a little while, quiet, looking happy,
her tasks done well, good things for those she loves.
I do not think it matters how old the universe will ever be.

A SIMPLE MEAL

She brought out two white plates,
sliced red tomatoes, a sprinkle of salt,
chunk of red cheese divided in two,
cold Black Forest ham cut
from the leftover haunch
of a bigger feast. This is better.
She added red berries for the sweet;
glasses of red wine clinked together.
Two of us in deep evening shade,
birds still flying below red clouds,
scent of jasmine tingeing the air.
We sat quiet, not talking much.
Behind us the house is brightly lit;
the laughter of young people reaches us.
We raise our glasses. We know something.

FORECAST

We are not what we fear we will become,
not yet anyway, not sad, not sick, not nothing.
I have risen with birdsong, strong and healthy
"for my age", as old men proudly claim.
You have arranged the flowers, made the coffee.
We sit and talk about the day to come.
Old Cameron, the gardener, will bring his gold papaws,
tell us about his harvest with pleasure in his voice.
We know the grand-children are visiting;
exchanging stories about them we laugh into each other's eyes.
It's hard, but we avoid the hate in the headlines.
There are so many ways to love this world.
Outside we will walk amidst the red blaze of poinsettias,
the music of the wind in the tall trees.
Let me say the earth is giving a good account of itself
today and tomorrow and as long as we want to think.
We forget completely what the old priest's sermon said:
All beauty raised on high will also be thrown down.

SUNSET

Coming home, late evening from a children's party,
Jacob saw them first, called "Look, look!" in wonder.
A flash of scarlet ibis landed in a nearby field –
tall grass growing between silvery pools of water –
in such numbers they made a lake of blood.
Rarely, very rarely, does Heaven show such wares.
Some sudden signal, the flash rose as one.
Now there was this new wonder to behold:
what victory, what Heavenly ascension!
Sunset flew up from earth to decorate the sky.

JACOB AND THE MOTH

"Why do moths try to kill themselves
flying round the lamp?" my grandson asks.
"Jacob, it is not death they seek,
it is their sun they want to reach.
Life would be worth it if they could."
"But they would die if they succeed."
"That is true; we must think about it.
Do we prefer to live or dying reach the sun?"
"Well, I'd prefer to live and just look at the sun."
"Sensible, I have to say. Jacob, you are right."
Ah what great cause I smile and think
may one day come to claim him?

A DEATH IN THE FAMILY

Forty years it stood from shrub to splendour,
the almond tree my wife planted now cut down;
green-branched beauty all dismembered,
the deadly whining noise of the electric saw
shrieking when it hit hard knots of wood –
bone in its flesh. It made us shudder.
When we married she planted it with love,
but the tree was ruled a foot or so illegal.
Our neighbour said, Too much, too much,
the roots would spoil his prestige driveway.
The city engineer's edict must be executed,
so our lovely tree was torn asunder.
All gone that wonder of green foliage
in which bright parrots flew and caterwauled,
the green leaves in the sun at dawn
signalling another day of familiar beauty.
In its stately shade I read a thousand books,
toasted births and victories with wine.
In season, its leaves took on red and golden tints,
dropped like royal caps in rich profusion –
grandchildren made of them masks for carnival.
And when the moon was full and risen
a lantern of great beauty shone amidst the branches.
How we will miss our wind and moon-entangled
almond tree, the whole sky empty where it stood.
City Hall records: a job completed.

THE PATTERN IN THE WEAVE

I notice the rush of the tall clouds,
as if a great fire was set far away;
heard how the hawks scream in the trees
louder than normal. A blood moon,
supposed to be rare, sails
continuously in the night sky.
Have you seen the luxurious growth of flowers?
Do you remember a few weeks ago
how fireflies fell and tangled in your hair,
a strange and beautiful nestling,
music just beyond the reach of hearing?
And today – I cannot recall it ever happening
before – deep sorrow graven on your face.

THE FUTURE NEVER HAPPENS

Walking with Cassandra along the darkening river
she knows so well, she said to me,
"The future never happens."
I kept silent, not understanding what she meant.
Dark clouds scudded before a rising wind,
casting shadows, spreading silvery maps.
"So beautiful," she said, "the last light of day.
The future never happens," she said again.
Silence grew around us, except the rising wind.
I thought I understood what she meant.

LIGHTNING FLASH

Storm coming, wild gusts of wind
hitting the trees, rain in the air.
Out in the garden in old clothes –
worth seeing a big storm at night.
Thunder's huge lorries roll in the distance;
silver vase shatters in the far low cloud.
Had I blinked at that particular moment –
eyelids closing just then to keep out light –
I would have missed unusual beauty.
Lightning made pitchforks in the night
like three-pronged candelabra tall as men
in old cathedral naves seen long ago.
I remember hot wax in the white cups.

SONG

I woke this morning,
a bird was singing its heart out.
Every morning there is birdsong.
Yes, but that wasn't this song;
this went on a long time.
It made me lie awake
and memories hurt me.
Never heard this before,
never heard this birdsong.
Where have you gone
the song said,
where have you gone?

THE MORNING

A good, ordinary morning starting with thunder,
crack of sound in the distance, though the sun shone
brilliantly through the window by my bed.
Wind also poured in, frangipani-tinted, from the sea.
In the kitchen, Mary was making coffee and cheese omelette;
humming a song, she fixed marigolds in a red pot
on the breakfast table, brought in green ferns.
I went out on the verandah to look at the garden:
a glorious morning, everything freshened and green.
There are such times – no hurt in body or mind,
surrounded by small perfections, a loving person near.
"A set of green parrots just flew by," Mary reported.
That's a good sign, they haven't come here for months,
camouflaging in the green tree's crown, caterwauling.
I've missed them. Perhaps all of Nature is coming back.

Over the front door, George Simon's wondrous painting
shines – *Essequibo Lit by the Dawn Sun* –
a sweeping vision of red and gold cast over the great river.
I note the small, gold-coloured Correia ceramic bowl,
decorated with an Amerindian universe of Gods.
It fell a while back, broke into bright pieces.
"I'm going to fix it today", she said, and she will.
She is orderer, repairer, minder, carer –
not much she can't restore, until the heart breaks.
I place my hand gently on my chest; all is well for now.
On the road outside a lady sells her wares;
she came walking, a huge basket balanced on her head.
What a feat, I thought, what hard practice to be so marvellous.
She had fresh-dug tannias for sale. I love tannias
roasted and crisp; I hadn't tasted them for a long time.
"We'll have tannia cakes tonight and I'll make a Caesar's salad."
If all this was not enough, the grandchildren are coming,
Zoey dancing in delight over everything in her life,

Jacob smiling and solemn. I want to discuss
his latest saying: "There is beauty in not knowing."
How did that come across his mind when he heard
his parents say the earth still holds many mysteries?

SADNESS

The white rose fades
petals on a red floor
beautiful pattern
has to be swept up
replaced

WHAT HAPPENS AFTERWARDS – ALL THE TIME

Ah what a deluge of happenings in my life.
In the white stone birdbath, blue sakis flirt.
Kenneth the yard man brings orchids to the door,
gold sun-bursts in his calloused hand.
How pleased he seems to have found such beauty.
Blue Mountain brewing will taste of home and comfort.
My wife kisses me on the lips for some good reason.
Jacob has been explaining why whales don't die of cancer.
He says, "Granddad, you are never too old to learn."
The corner of my ear hears distant thunder;
at some deep level I feel galaxies spin.
No doubt the soul is all the while considering eternity.
This time last week I slipped on the polished floor;
where I am now, blood flowed from a cracked skull.

EXILE

Old Ganesh has an upcurving white moustache,
tweaks it with a flourish, unconscious of himself.
He brought us baskets of greens and red tomatoes,
purple-skinned sweet potatoes, fresh from the earth.
His home garden up the East Coast never failed
while all these years his moustache turned from black to white.
Always that flourish made me smile.
Sunday, early, he comes strangely to our back door.
"They send to bring us, our sons. USA tickets come."
He brought a gift – a big basket of purple sweet potatoes.
Mary told him they were perfect for our Sunday soup.
Thanks, Ganesh. I looked him in his eyes; tears in mine too.

MAN WITH CUTLASS

A young man at the gate, barefoot, dishevelled,
thickly-bearded, wild-looking dreadlocks,
carrying a sack in the hot afternoon,
long cutlass held bare in his hand,
rattled the locked gate to get attention.
I looked out the window. What to think?
What to do? Call the police?
Message from the yardman: Nothing bad,
the man was thirsty, could he get water?
He had his own cup as he showed.
I sent out a jug of cold tap water;
he filled his cup twice and drank deep,
saluted thanks, and slowly went his way.
Oh God, wish I could be a better person.

REMNANTS OF THE DAY

When I went over today in my mind,
quite a few good and bad things happened.
The flamboyants are in brilliant full colour,
and it's always good to talk and laugh with my wife,
but my nagging toothache got slightly worse
and my tax return is due, yet for some reason
what is most vivid – I cracked and shelled
a bag of walnuts – a pile of broken shells
on the green tablecloth; sweet kernels
filling only a small bowl.

LIFE'S SHARP TURNING POINTS

An insistent early morning phone –
so early very rarely happens.
Can we contact Mary? The doctor's message.
We have the result of the mammogram.
Can she speak? I hear wild geese heavy overhead;
they must be beautiful, I think.
I'm her husband. I can take the call.
Hesitation. Then the message: normal

THE MOON AND THE MOTH

A hard wind blew all day and strengthened;
it stripped leaves, young twigs from the trees.
At night, a huge white moon arose;
carved from ice, it raced across the sky
as dark clouds drove the other way.
Watching that great ice moon from my study,
its wild beauty wondrous to my eyes,
I noted a black moth beating on the window;
again, again, it battered on the pane,
deep blue gleaming on winged blackness,
a thing so beautiful wanting to escape,
fly out and soar along the racing moon.
Let go, it could not ride the wind,
its wings becoming leaves falling in the night.

CAMP-FIRE

I went to bed earlier than my wife –
she was making finishing touches
to her cross-stitch pattern,
listening contentedly to the music –
Pavarotti ascending to where angels sing.
I was cold when she came up,
moved near her, my camp-fire,
put my hand out to touch her face.
"Love you," she said. "Love you, too."
"Sleep well until morning light" –
something she often says.
I don't anymore, but of course
that's not the point. I woke as usual
sometime later, her dark hair
scattered wildly – saw it was as I remember.

THE ARRIVAL OF HAPPINESS

Late morning rain coming down heavily,
sky black-clouded, horizon to horizon.
Not the sort of day for exaltations.
There was an open-air jazz concert later
I would have enjoyed – cancelled, of course.
Anyway, my wife bought us cups of coffee,
the veranda green with hanging ferns around us,
orchids in a bowl, a Greaves painting we loved.
Two pure white egrets surprised us,
flags waving past, landed with a splash.
I stood loving the rain, elegant garden, artwork,
the coffee, my wife there, sudden beauty, life.

A NIGHT NOT QUITE WITHOUT A MOON

I went out to watch the stars in purest night,
hoping to see their sharpened brightness,
to see them glitter, sparks of white fire.
Lucky, it was night of moving clouds. Moonlight
pales the stars; you can almost see through them,
its brilliance making them dull spots.
Tonight they are gleaming, fire-glints in dark water –
a black princess wearing her necklace of best pearls.
Just before going in, something caught my inner eye.
Tucked in one corner of the bowl of night, the thinnest
curve of light, a fingernail most delicately pared;
a crescent hardly there, more beautiful than any star.

ABOUT THE AUTHOR

Ian McDonald was born in Trinidad April 18th 1933. He was educated at Queens Royal College, Guyana and Clare College, Cambridge University (1951-55). In 1955 he joined Bookers in the then British Guiana, and spent 52 years in the sugar industry, becoming Director of Marketing & Administration with Bookers and continuing with GuySuCo after nationalization in 1976, until 1999. Between 2000 – 2007 he was CEO of the Sugar Association of the Caribbean. He was an Editorial Consultant with the West Indian Commission, 1991-92. In January 2009 he was appointed Chairman of Guyana Publications Inc., publishers of *Stabroek News*.

As a lawn tennis player he played at Wimbledon, captained Cambridge, Guyana and the West Indian Davis Cup team in the 1960s. He was Guyana's Sportsman of the Year in 1957.

He has published seven poetry collections (*Mercy Ward*, *Essequibo*, *Jaffo the Calypsonian*, *Between Silence and Silence*, *Selected Poem*, *The Comfort of All Things*, *River Dancer* and *Collected Poems*), and prose collections of essays and speeches, *A Cloud of Witnesses* and *A Love of Poetry*. His novel *The Humming-Bird Tree* was published in 1969 and was made into a BBC film in 1992. He won the Guyana Prize for Literature – for poetry – in 1992, 2004, and 2012. He edited the magazine *Kyk-Over-Al* from 1984 to 2000. He edited: *AJS at 70: The Collected Poems of A.J. Seymour* with Jacqueline de Weever and *The Heinemann Book of Caribbean Poetry in English,* with Stewart Brown; with Lloyd Searwar, Joel Benjamin and Laxshmi Kallicharan he contributed to compiling *They Came in Ships*, an anthology of Indo-Guyanese writing and he edited *The Bowling Was Superfine*, an anthology of West Indian cricket writing, with Stewart Brown. In 2008 his *Selected Poems* was shortlisted for the Royal Society of Literature Ondaatje Literary Prize. His one-act play, *The Tramping Man*, produced in Guyana in 1969, was published by UWI's School of Continuing Studies in *A Time and a Season: 8 Caribbean Plays*. His weekly column, "Ian on Sunday" has appeared in *Stabroek News* for thirty years.

He has written extensively on cricket and in 2005 delivered the

Inaugural Lecture entitled "Cricket: A Hunger in the West Indian Soul" in the Sir Frank Worrell lecture series. He was a member of a panel set up by the West Indies Cricket Board in 2007 to report and make recommendations on the governance of West Indies Cricket. He assisted in the compilation and production of *Cricket At Bourda*, celebrating the Georgetown Cricket Club, in time for the World Cup, March 2007.

He was elected a Fellow of the Royal Society of Literature in 1970, received the Golden Arrow of Achievement Guyana national award (1986) and in 1997 the University of the West Indies conferred on him an Honorary Doctorate of Letters for services to sugar, sport and literature. He contributed, with his sister Robin McDonald, to the publication of their mother's memoir, *Beloved, Memoir by Thelma Seheult*, published by Paria Publishing in Trinidad, 2016, and also to their father's memoir, *Archie, the Memoir. An Abounding Joy*, a collection of essays on cricket and sport, edited by Professor Clem Seecharan was published by Hansib in 2018. He and his wife, Mary Angela, have two sons, Jamie and Darren, and he has a son Keith from a previous marriage.

ALSO BY IAN McDONALD

New and Collected Poems
ISBN: 9781845234034; pp. 448; pub. 2018; price £17.99

From the earliest poems published in the 1950s, Ian McDonald has been a distinctive and admired voice in Caribbean poetry. This volume brings together all his published collections: *Jaffo the Calypsonian*, *Mercy Ward*, *Essequibo*, *Between Silence and Silence*, *The Comfort of All Things* and *River Dancer*. In addition, there are almost two books' worth of new poems, the product of a remarkable flowering of inspiration and memory that visited Ian McDonald in his eighties.

The poems reflect both a changing Caribbean world and changes in the witnessing self, though there are consistencies of vision. Few Caribbean poets have so sensuously observed the region's natural world, but have also been aware of the dangers of the "gilding eye" glossing over the poverty which is still the lot of so many Caribbean people. Poems celebrate the pleasures of good company, love, marriage, children, food, gardens and books, but set against this the knowledge that whilst his has been a life that has contributed much to the good of the region, it has also been one of the privilege of material security and whiteness. Many poems display a compassionate concern with the suffering of Guyana's poor, particularly in the stark realism of the *Mercy Ward* poems.

There is also an inward eye, aware of the passing years. From the son who sees his parents' ageing, the father of growing children, the keen sportsman facing the decline of middle age, and the man facing his own later years of health anxieties, though nourished by a loving wife, attentive grandchildren and the pleasures of the garden. All these phases of life return to the poetry of the past few years.